INTERNET
PIONEERS

The *Collective Biographies* Series

Collective Biographies

INTERNET PIONEERS
The Cyber Elite

Laura French

Enslow Publishers, Inc.

40 Industrial Road   PO Box 38
Box 398   Aldershot
Berkeley Heights, NJ 07922   Hants GU12 6BP
USA   UK

http://www.enslow.com

Library of Congress Cataloging-in-Publication Data

French, Laura, 1949 –
    Internet pioneers : The Cyber Elite / Laura French.
        p. cm. — (Collective biographies)
    Includes bibliographical references (p.) and index.
    Includes biographies of Andrew Grove, Lawrence Ellison, Ann Winblad, Esther
Dyson, Steve Jobs, William H. Gates, Steve Case, Jeffrey P. Bezos, Jerry Yang, and
Linus Torvalds.
    ISBN 0-7660-1540-8
    1. Internet—Biography—Juvenile literature. 2.Businesspeople—Biography—
Juvenile literature. [1. Internet. 2. Businesspeople. 3. Computer industry.]
I. Title. II. Series.
TK5105.875.I57 F7745   2001
004'.092'2—dc21
                                                    00-011117

Printed in the United States of America

10 9 8 7 6 5 4 3 2 1

To Our Readers:
All Internet Addresses in this book were active and appropriate when we went to press.
Any comments or suggestions can be sent by e-mail to Comments@enslow.com or to
the address on the back cover.

Illustration Credits: AP/Wide World Photos, p. 94; © 2000, Edventure
Holdings, Inc., pp. 38, 45; Courtesy of America Online, Inc., pp. 68, 74;
Courtesy of Amazon, p. 82; Courtesy of Apple Computer, Inc.,
p. 53; Courtesy of Hummer Winblad Venture Partners, pp. 30, 35; Courtesy
of Intel Corporation, pp. 12, 17; Courtesy of Linux, p. 99; Courtesy of
Microsoft Corporation, pp. 58, 64; Courtesy of NeXT Software, Inc., p. 48;
Courtesy of Oracle Corporation, pp. 20, 27; The Seattle Times, p. 78;
yahoo! inc., pp. 86, 91.

Cover Illustration: Courtesy of Hummer Winblad Venture Partners;
Courtesy of Microsoft Corporation; Courtesy of Oracle Corporation;
yahoo! inc.

Contents

Preface

You know how fast things happen in cyberspace: You send an e-mail, and a friend in another city receives it minutes later. You log onto the Internet, and you retrieve information from anywhere in the world in a matter of seconds.

In the world of computer technology, change happens almost as fast. New developments make today's equipment obsolete, practically overnight. New companies spring up from nowhere, doing things that have never been done before. Other companies merge, are bought out, or fail and disappear.

So, by the time you read this book, some of the information in it is bound to be out of date. It is impossible to tell what will change, but it is interesting to speculate. As I write these pages, Transmeta Corporation has just introduced a new computer chip designed especially for mobile computing. If this chip catches on, cell phones and Palm Pilots may replace desktop computers as the most common way to send e-mail or surf the Internet. This one development could have a big impact on the futures of three of the people in this book. Linus Torvalds currently works for Transmeta. If his operating system, Linux, becomes the basis for mobile computing, it could threaten the dominance of Bill Gates' Microsoft Windows. And in order to succeed, Transmeta will have to compete with the world's chip-manufacturing giant, Intel, the company that Andrew Grove helped to found.

In the same month that Transmeta released its new chip, Microsoft unveiled its Windows 2000 operating system. It may help Microsoft compete with the Unix operating system on networked computers. Currently, Larry Ellison's Oracle Corporation dominates the Unix software market. So the long-standing rivalry between Ellison and Gates may now get even hotter. And once again, there is no telling what role Linus Torvald's Linux, the rebel operating system, may play. Will it remain the plaything of a small group of software developers? Or will it be adopted by masses of home and business users, ending the dominance of Windows?

As these examples show, change is inevitable, and it is impossible to predict exactly how cyberspace will evolve. It does seem likely, though, that the ten people profiled in this book will continue to be major contributors. For one thing, it is a world that they helped to create. Steve Jobs, Bills Gates, and Andrew Grove were present at the birth of the personal computer, and they saw its potential. Jobs founded Apple Computer, Bill Gates started Microsoft Corporation, and Andrew Grove made Intel the world's leading manufacturer of computer "chips." Ann Winblad, like Gates, knew that software, not hardware, would be the area of fastest growth. She founded her own software development company and sold it for a small fortune. Then she became a venture capitalist, helping other young entrepreneurs get their ideas off the ground. Larry Ellison understood that businesses, like individuals, would want to replace the cumbersome mainframe computer with something more flexible. His Oracle software paved the way for client/server technology. Less than 20 years later, Jerry Yang and Steve Case witnessed the birth of the Internet, and developed applications that made it useful for millions of people. Yang and his partner David Filo founded Yahoo, and Case made e-mail easy with America Online (AOL). Jeff Bezos spotted the emerging wave of "e-commerce" and helped make it a reality with Amazon.com. Esther Dyson nurtured creative thinking about technology with her publication *Release 1.0*. Linus Torvalds saw that the huge profits to be made from computer technology might actually limit quality and innovation, and offered an alternative: the Linux operating system, developing using code that everyone could contribute to.

Each of these people had the insight to recognize a turning point in cyber-history. And each of them had the ability to create the product or service that was needed at that moment.

Just as important, all ten of these cyber-pioneers are still very much involved in the future direction of their companies and their specialized fields. Only Andrew Grove has reached retirement age. The other people profiled here have ten, twenty, or even thirty or more year's left in the workplace. None of these pioneers show any sign of slowing down. Grove's age and health problems have not stopped him from being a fierce competitor. Being the richest man in the world does not seem to stop Bill Gates. Steve Jobs was fired from Apple Computer and came back stronger than ever as head of not one but two successful technology companies.

The fast-paced computer world does cause burn out. Steve Wozniak, who co-founded Apple with Steve Jobs, retired as a millionaire and now teaches computing to elementary school children. David Filo, who co-founded Yahoo, recently announced his plans to return to Stanford University and finish his studies. Although he continues to share the title of "Head Yahoo" with Jerry Yang, he may not be as visible or as involved in the company.

But more often, it seems, one success leads to another. Or perhaps these ten people were just born with the ability to "think different," as the Apple Computer advertisement campaign urges. They continue to have new and different thoughts about technology. By thinking different, they have helped to change the world. It seems likely that they will continue to be creators of change for many tomorrows.

Andrew Grove

Chairman of the Board, Intel

In Spring 1999, tens of thousands of people were fleeing their homes in Kosovo, Yugoslavia. The International Rescue Committee, which was helping to provide food, clothing, and shelter, received a donation of $150,000 from Andy Grove. As the chairman of Intel, Grove is head of "the most profitable manufacturing company on the planet."[1] He is also someone who knows firsthand what it is like to be a penniless political refugee.

Andy Grove was born András Gróf in Hungary on September 2, 1936. He and his family are Jewish. When the Nazis conquered Hungary during World War II, his father, George, was forced into a work brigade and then was sent away to war. His wife and children did not know where he was. Young András

Andrew Grove

and his mother, Maria, had to go into hiding. Some of his relatives were found and sent to concentration camps, where many of them died. Those are the years that Grove's two daughters call "what Dad doesn't talk about."[2]

Things did not get much better after the war. Hungary came under the control of the Soviet Union. It was an oppressive regime, where freedom of thought and speech were restricted.

Worried about his safety, twenty-year-old András Gróf decided to escape from Hungary. He and a friend bought directions from a smuggler for leaving the country. They crawled through the mud to the Austrian border, while soldiers patrolled nearby. No wonder Grove's motto has been, "Only the paranoid survive!"

In spite of his new, American-sounding name, Andrew Grove hardly spoke a word of English when he arrived in New York. The International Rescue Committee (IRC) sent him to a dentist and helped him get a hearing aid. Treatment for his dental and hearing problems were neglected because of the war. Grove still has the small paper tag that was stuck on his lapel by an IRC worker when he arrived.

He lived with his uncle in the Bronx and enrolled at the City College of New York where he studied chemical engineering. He received a scholarship, but he also worked as a waiter to pay his expenses. At one of those jobs, at a summer resort in the Catskill

Mountains, he met another young Hungarian. Her name was Eva, and she soon became his wife.

In spite of studying in a foreign language, Grove worked hard and graduated at the top of his class. His high grades let him choose among many graduate schools. He chose the University of California at Berkeley to get away from New York's cold winters. By 1963, Grove earned his Ph.D. He took a job working in research at Fairchild Semiconductor and continued to lecture at Berkeley. Semiconductors are materials with special properties. They have made possible modern computers and other important electronic devices.

Grove's brilliant mind soon made him a leading expert in semiconductors. In 1967, he even wrote a book on the subject, *Physics and Technology of Semiconductor Devices*, that has been used in many university courses. When Robert Noyce and Gordon Moore left Fairchild in 1968 to start their own company, Intel, they invited Andy Grove to come along. Grove was made director of operations. His job was to be sure that Intel's products were made on time and within the budget. Although his background was scientific research, not manufacturing, Grove's love of detail made him perfect for his new job. When the company was starting up, he found and leased the first office and factory space and he ordered the first telephones.

Grove approached his new job like a scientist. He wanted every aspect of the company to be measurable, so he would know whether changes made things better or worse. He thought the accounts payable department should keep track of the number of vouchers they processed. The janitors should count the number of square feet they cleaned.

To deal with problems in the company, Grove used a technique he called "constructive confrontation."[3] That meant people should be able to say what they thought, and others should not take it personally.

Sometimes, when Andy Grove said what was on his mind, people did take it personally. He once gave his secretary, Sue McFarland, such a bad performance review that she burst into tears.[4] One year, Grove was irritated because a number of employees left the office early on the day before the Christmas holiday. The next year, he sent around a memo reminding them that they had to work until the normal quitting time. Intel employees called this "the Scrooge memo."[5]

But Andy Grove did not just handle the small details at Intel. He also helped set the direction of the company. In 1978, Intel was facing serious competition from Motorola. Some people said the Motorola 68000 microprocessor was better, faster, cheaper, and easier to use than Intel's 8086. Grove developed a program called "Operation Crush" to beat the competition. Intel emphasized its wider product line, better trained sales force, and better customer service. By the end of 1980, Intel had become the market leader.

15

By 1985, however, Intel faced another challenge. One of the company's original product lines, the dynamic random-access memory (DRAM) chip was facing fierce competition from Japan. The Japanese manufacturers were actually willing to sell their chips for less than it cost to manufacture them just to stay in the fight. It was hard for Intel to think about getting out of the memory chip market, where they had been leaders for so long. Finally, Andy Grove asked Gordon Moore the crucial question: "If we got kicked out, and the board brought in a new CEO, what do you think he would do?" Moore said a new CEO would undoubtedly get out of the memory chip business. Grove asked, "Why shouldn't you and I walk out the door, come back and do it ourselves?"[6]

To get out of the memory chip business, Intel had to fire more than five thousand employees. The company also had to gamble that their other product lines, including processors for the new personal computer market, would be popular enough to support the company. The gamble paid off for Andy Grove and for Intel. In 1987, Grove was made CEO of the company. By 1999, the company's sales were eight times higher than they were when Grove took over. The cost of a share of stock was twenty-four times higher. Most of that growth has come from its processor chips—386, 486, Pentium I, Pentium II, and Pentium III. The chips have made Intel famous while dramatically improving the performance of personal computers.

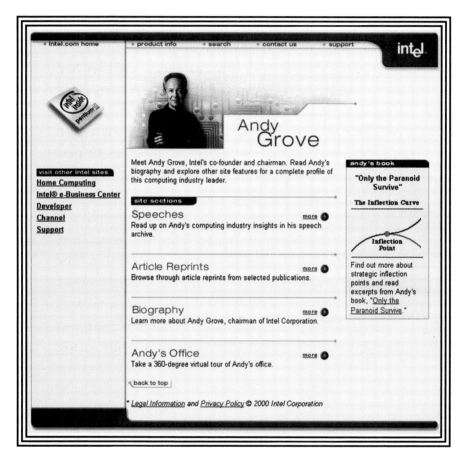

Andy Grove started as director of operations at Intel in 1968. He is now chairman of the board.

But it was not all smooth sailing. When Intel first introduced its Pentium chip in 1994, it had a very small flaw. Only a few specialized users would even notice the flaw, which would only affect very complex problems in long division. But the news media started to publish stories about Intel's bad chip. IBM, which used thousands of Intel chips, put its orders on hold. Finally, Andy Grove issued a public apology—for the flaw in the Pentium chip and for Intel's failure to take its customers seriously. He announced that Intel would replace any flawed chip for free. The company set aside $475 million to cover the costs. Grove later said that his refusal to replace the chips immediately was "my biggest mistake."[7]

Just a year later, Grove faced what may have been his biggest personal challenge when his doctor told him he had prostate cancer. Grove soon discovered that there were many contradictory theories about how to treat his form of cancer. "I also decided to dust off my research background," he said later. He read different scientific papers and compared the data. The process of learning, he said, "added a strange element of enjoyment to a process that was, overall, very scary."[8]

His research convinced him that surgical removal of his prostate was not a good idea. Instead, he had "smart bombs" of radioactive material placed inside his body, next to the tumors. Every day for twenty-eight days, he went to the hospital at 7:30 A.M., had a radiation treatment, then went to work. So far, the treatment seems to have been successful. But Grove said, "I know I will be stuck with this fear for the rest of my life."[9]

On May 1, 1999, Andy Grove stepped down as CEO of Intel. Rumors started that his cancer was back. But Grove explained that he wanted his successor, Craig Barrett, to have some time to run Intel. "He's paid his dues and has lots of ideas," Grove explained.[10]

Perhaps Grove also wanted to enjoy his other interests. He goes skiing, bikes with his wife Eva, and listens to the opera. He teaches an annual course at Stanford University's business school that students clamor to get into. He has a close relationship with his two daughters, whose names and occupations he asks the media not to reveal.[11]

Grove is hardly retired. He stayed on as chairman of the board, a job that would allow him to remain a public figure and stay active in the company. "We built the guts of modern computing, period," Andy Grove said. "We'll go away when modern computing goes away."[12] He seemed to be speaking both for his company and for himself.

Lawrence Ellison

Lawrence Ellison

President and CEO, Oracle Corporation

Every year, there is a boat race from Sydney, Australia to Hobart, Tasmania which are 630 nautical miles apart. The boats sail along the coastline of Australia, then cross the open seas of the Southern Ocean. In 1995, Larry Ellison entered his yacht, *Sayonara*, in the race. "There's nothing to stop the wind, and there's nothing to stop the waves. So they just get bigger and bigger and bigger," Ellison recalled. "You've got double lifelines on; you can't move on the deck without clipping into one thing, unclipping from something else. . . . If you have to go down below to the bathroom, you have to take all your clothes off. And you can't take your clothes off without being thrown around the boat because you're hitting these waves. . . . You just hope to be able to go to the bathroom and not break an arm or a leg or be knocked unconscious into a coma." The *Sayonara* had the best crew he could hire. Even so, Ellison recalled that two thirds of the crew were throwing up. "We smelled pretty bad and looked worse when we finally got to Hobart," Ellison said. But the *Sayonara* was the first American boat to win the race in seventeen years.[1]

That boat race reveals two important things about Larry Ellison: He likes to win, and he does not mind taking risks. The same two traits helped Ellison build Oracle Software into the second-largest software company in the world. And they have helped him rise from poverty to become one of the richest men in the United States.

If Lawrence Joseph Ellison had not been a fighter, he might not have survived. He was born on August 17, 1944. His mother, Florence, was only nineteen years old. She was alone, but she tried to keep the baby. When he almost died of pneumonia, she decided that he needed a better life. She gave the baby to her aunt Lillian Ellison. Lillian and her husband, Louis, adopted the baby. Until he was twelve years old, Ellison did not know he was adopted. He did not know who his birth mother was until much later. "I think it's very difficult to be that different, to wonder if you belong to your own family," he said.[2]

Louis Ellison was a Russian immigrant who took his last name from Ellis Island, where many

European immigrants landed when they came to America. He settled in Chicago, worked hard and became a wealthy landlord. Then, came the Great Depression, a time when thousands of people were left with no jobs, no money, no homes, and no food. Louis Ellison lost all his money. Lawrence Ellison recalled that the south side of Chicago, where he was raised, was "a Jewish ghetto." But, he said, "I did not even know I lived in a 'bad' neighborhood. I was unaware of it. No one told me. And I did not discover it until I left."[3]

Even as a boy, Ellison insisted on doing things his own way. He refused to go through the bar mitzvah ceremony at age thirteen. While his friends had their hair cut at home by their fathers, Ellison went to a professional barber. He preferred show tunes to the rock and roll that was becoming popular with teenagers. And, although he loved to play basketball, he was not cut out for teamwork. Instead, he shot baskets at the YMCA.

When he graduated from high school in 1962, Ellison enrolled at the University of Illinois at Urbana-Champaign. Then, at the end of his sophomore year, Lillian Ellison died of cancer. "I just left without taking finals," he recalled. "I never went back."[4] Ellison enrolled at the University of Chicago. In a physics class, he was required to program an IBM computer. "I just picked up a book and started programming," he said. "I never took a computer science class in my life."[5] Soon, Ellison was working as a computer programmer. Although he later claimed to have a degree in physics from the university, the records show that he was only enrolled for one semester. Then he left for Berkeley, California, driving a bright blue Ford Thunderbird.[6]

In California, Ellison met and fell in love with Adda Quinn. They were married in January 1967. Although they saved up enough money to buy a house, Ellison moved from one job to another, with no real idea of how he was going to spend his life. He bought himself an expensive bicycle and an even more expensive sailboat. It was up to his wife to balance the budget. By 1974, Adda had had enough. She was developing an ulcer. She told Ellison she wanted to leave him. "He said to me, 'If you stay with me, I will become a millionaire and you can have anything you want,'" Adda Quinn recalled.[7] She thought it was a laughable promise, coming from a man who had no ambition and no plans for a career. Adda Quinn divorced Larry Ellison. But his promise was a turning point.

In 1977, Ellison convinced two friends to form a company to go after a software contract at the company where Ellison was working. They called the new company Software Development Laboratories (SDL). Because it was Ellison's idea to form the company, he bought 60 percent of the stock. His two partners bought 20 percent each.

While SDL was being paid by Ellison's former company, the SDL programmers were spending most of their time working on a project of their own. It was a new kind of software product called a relational database system. The theory of relational databases had been developed ten years before, but nobody had tried to turn the theory into reality. People thought that relational software could not be made fast enough to be commercial. Ellison thought that he could prove them wrong.

Ellison and his partners finally stopped their consulting work so they could concentrate full-time on their new product, Oracle. They had $200,000 saved up from their consulting contract. They made that money last for two years, while they wrote the code for Oracle. In November 1979, the first version of Oracle was sold and installed. Larry Ellison spent five weeks on the road doing the installation and training the users.

Ellison had been married a second time, to Nancy Elizabeth Wheeler. Eighteen months later, just about the time Larry Ellison's company was taking off, his marriage was breaking up.

The early versions of Oracle software were not very reliable. Ellison, who is a pilot as well as a sailboat enthusiast, said his product was like the fastest airplanes: "occasionally the wings fall off. So make sure you have a parachute."[8] But, somehow, customers did not seem to mind.

In 1981, Ellison hired an office receptionist named Barbara Booth. The two flirted over the company's e-mail system. They dated, moved in together, and had a son, David. Booth told Ellison that she wanted to marry Ellison before their son was a year old. Eleven months later, they were married. Their second child, a daughter, named Margaret Elizabeth, nicknamed Megan, was born in January 1986.

But, by that time, Ellison's company, which had changed its name to Oracle Corporation, was about to make its initial public stock offering. Because of this, Ellison was rarely home and he had no time to work on the problems in his marriage. In April 1986, he filed for divorce.

Ellison pushed hard for more sales of the Oracle product in those early years. His critics said he was trying to make the company grow too fast. Ellison retorted that only the top one or two companies selling a particular product or service can be sure to make a profit. He wanted Oracle to be at the top.[9]

Still, it seemed for a while as though Ellison was losing interest in Oracle. While other chief executive officers like Bill Gates and Jerry Yang worked round the clock, Ellison worked only about 50 hours a week. He went to the office so rarely that his visits were called "Elvis sightings."[10]

Some of his outside interests were risky for a man at the head of a growing company. In addition to racing his yacht, Ellison flies his own plane. He taught his son, David, to fly when he was thirteen years old. Ellison shattered his elbow during a bike race and broke his neck and punctured a lung while body surfing in Hawaii. Even Ellison's good friend Steve

Larry Ellison was among the first business leaders to spot the importance of the Internet.

Jobs called Ellison the "outrageous CEO poster child."[11]

But when sales began to lag in the mid-1990s, Larry Ellison's competitive drive seemed to be reborn. Ellison was among the first business leaders to spot the importance of the Internet. Oracle developed new versions of its relational software that store data on an Internet "server" rather than on the user's desktop computer. Ellison even believes that the NC, or network computer, will soon replace the PC, or personal computer.

By 1999, Oracle was worth 8 billion dollars. In June 2000, *Red Herring Magazine* named Oracle Corporation one of its "Top 50 Public Companies." The magazine reported that Oracle's applications are "once again taking the new economy by storm." Noting Ellison's renewed commitment to his company, *Red Herring* said, "Thrill-seeking CEO has stopped sailing around the world and is actually rumored to be putting in full days of work."[12]

Ellison still seems determined to enjoy life. He drives expensive cars. He wears "double-breasted suits, French cuffs and knuckle-size cuff links." He is building a new, $40 million home that looks like a sixteenth-century Japanese palace.[13] But these days he is putting business first. In Ellison's mind, the software industry is a two-man race: Larry Ellison versus Bill Gates. It is a race that Larry Ellison wants to win.

As his friend KC Branscomb has said, "Larry believes in strength, and the swift and effective exercising of power. In his view, he's just rising to the top of the food chain in the same way that a lion doesn't think too much about the antelope it takes in the bush for dinner."[14]

Ann Winblad

Ann Winblad
Venture Capitalist

When Ann Winblad was a little girl, she made Barbie doll clothes and sold them to her friends at school. She recalls that she "made a ton of money selling these things pretty cheap." Winblad thinks she would have done even better if the Internet had existed when she was a kid. "But if I had had the Web or could have built my own Internet site, I probably never would have gone to college, 'cause I would have been rich selling those Barbie doll clothes."[1]

Today, of course, the Internet is the fastest growing area of American business. And Ann Winblad's company, Hummer Winblad, Inc., invests money in young software companies in hopes that their ideas will make millions. The companies they have invested in include Liquid Audio, a company that makes software for sending music over the Internet, and The Knot, a Website that lets couples plan their weddings and order everything they need online.

Compared to Bill Gates and Steve Jobs, Ann Winblad was late in discovering the world of computers. She was born on November 1, 1950 in Farmington, Minnesota. The schools in her small hometown did not have computers let alone courses in operating or programming them. But Winblad kept busy with other things. In grade school, she "read every book in the library."[2] In high school, she showed that it was possible to be popular and be a good student at the same time. She was a cheerleader and the valedictorian of her senior class.

Her good grades got her into a small private college in St. Paul, Minnesota called the College of St. Catherine. Her college and its brother college, St. Thomas, had many computers that a local business had donated. "Once I figured out that there was such a thing as a computer and that programming was so much fun, I was cornered," Winblad recalled.[3]

When Winblad graduated, she was one of the few women in a high-demand field. She had her pick of jobs. She took one as a systems programmer for the Federal Reserve office in Minneapolis, Minnesota. The job paid very well for a new college graduate. Winblad worked in a new building in downtown Minneapolis. But the job was not demanding enough for Winblad. She recalls that one of her colleagues was gone everyday from 2 P.M. to 3 P.M. When Winblad finally asked him where he was going, he admitted that he went home to watch *I Dream of Jeannie* on television. Nobody ever missed him! "There was no commitment to build anything, no commitment to the products we were looking at," Winblad remembered.[4]

She wanted to start her own company. "I've got to do that. I'm going to program something, make it into a product, and sell it," she told herself.[5] She convinced three of her colleagues at the Federal Reserve to start it with her. Open Systems was incorporated in 1975. Their goal was to build a high-end accounting system for the new microcomputers that were coming into the market.

Like Apple and Microsoft, the new company was started on a shoestring: Each of the partners put in just five hundred dollars. To support themselves, they got a contract to build software for a local school district. At night they worked on their own software product. "Even my own parents said, 'You'll get over this,'" Winblad recalls.[6] But twenty-five years later, Winblad is still an entrepreneur, and she is encouraging others to become entrepreneurs as well.

Winblad had quit her job at the Federal Reserve to start the new company. Her three partners, on the other hand, just took one-year sabbaticals. At the end of the first year, the company had lost eighty-five dollars. That left her partners "slightly panicked."[7] But in reality that was a good result for the first year of a new business. In 1983, the partners sold their company for $15.1 million dollars.

After the company sold, Winblad spent a couple of years working as a consultant to leading computer companies like Apple, IBM, and Microsoft. She met another young entrepreneur about her own age and began to date him. Although the romance broke up, Winblad and Bill Gates are still good friends. In fact, they still spend one week a year alone together, sharing ideas.

"She brings a sense of enjoyment and humor to even the most serious situations. When Ann has a great insight, she'll explain it like it's simple common sense," Bill Gates says. "She is incredibly smart. Although she doesn't impose her ideas on other people, she has the confidence to laugh in a friendly way when a poor investment or poor strategy is suggested."[8]

Another entrepreneur, John Hummer, wanted Winblad to go into business with him. "He started hounding me for a year and a half, and he won me over to become his partner and start this firm," Winblad said.[9] Hummer Winblad is a venture capital firm. "A venture capitalist is a person who invests money," explains Winblad. "Money, usually large pension funds and endowments—considered high-risk capital—in private companies, in our case

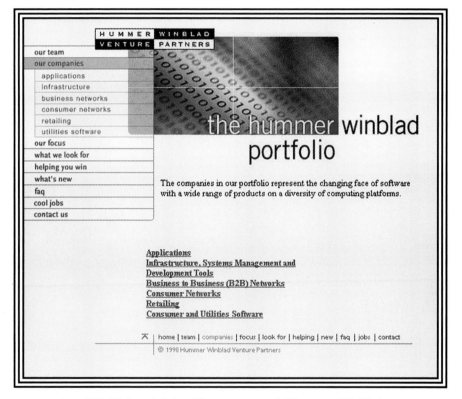

Ann Winblad and John Hummer started Hummer Winblad, a venture capital firm.

mostly startups. And what we do on a daily basis . . . is help build those companies from small companies into big companies."[10] Hummer Winblad has more than $200 million to invest in software companies. Their investments can range from under $100,000 up to $5 million.

John Hummer played basketball for the Seattle Supersonics before he became a venture capitalist. Maybe that is why Ann Winblad compares herself and her partner to "industry coaches." She says, "We form a professional coaching staff, and our job is to get software companies into the playoffs."[11]

Right from the beginning, Hummer and Winblad were determined to specialize in software companies. At the time, that seemed like a strange thing to do. But software had already made Ann Winblad a millionaire. She knew it could make money for other people, too. "Software is the centerpiece of the new economy," Winblad believes.[12]

Winblad knows that her position as a woman in the computer industry is unusual. Sometimes, she finds the interest in her gender annoying. For example, virtually every article on Winblad mentions her friendship with Bill Gates. Winblad does not think it would even be mentioned if she were "Bob Winblad."[13]

In general, though, Winblad finds being a woman in her industry to be "no problem." "In fact, I have all the advantage. In the next decade, when more women join venture capital firms, more women run software companies, they'll lose the unique position in the room that I have. It also puts a lot of responsibility on me. When people pay attention to you, you need to be articulate, you need to only talk about what you know. So there's responsibility but yes, I have a lot of benefit from being unique in the industry."[14]

Esther Dyson

Esther Dyson

President, EDventure Holdings, Inc.

Everyone who visits Esther Dyson's office notices how messy it is. One reporter made a list of the clutter that included "magazines, skin creams and lotions, mountains of newspapers, a plastic container of mayonnaise, teetering stacks of books, tote bags with damp bathing suits trailing out of them, a half-eaten chocolate bar, Russian nesting dolls, unopened CDs, four-year-old paychecks."[1]

Dyson has a simple explanation for the mess. "I don't have time to throw stuff away." "Esther works harder than anyone you'll ever meet," one of her friends said. "She'll be reading something when she walks down the street. She doesn't waste two seconds."[2] In the past ten years, she has only taken one vacation, which lasted for only four days.

Many people would be worn out by Dyson's pace. But she says, "I really like my life. I've never felt lonely on a Saturday night; I'd rather be alone than be bored."[3]

What keeps Esther Dyson so busy? That is harder to explain. She does not own a software company, like Bill Gates. She does not run a computer company, like Steve Jobs. She describes her career this way: "What I do is try to find worthy ideas and people and get attention for them."[4]

Esther Dyson publishes a newsletter called *Release 1.0*. A subscription costs hundreds of dollars a year, and only about fifteen hundred people subscribe. Those subscribers are the most important people in the world of computers, software, and Internet businesses. For the first four years, from 1984 to 1988, Dyson wrote every word of the newsletter herself.

She is a good and interesting writer, but her newsletter succeeds because she publishes farsighted ideas. More than ten years ago, she predicted that computer software would be distributed over the Internet. It was an amazing idea at the time. In her June 1990 newsletter, Dyson described the "HandyWidget," a handheld computer that people could use to take notes and keep track of appointments. Today, the personal data assistant (PDA) is becoming a popular item. "I'm always considered a crackpot because I'm early with ideas," Dyson said. "But that's O.K."[5]

Every year, Dyson puts on a conference called the PC Forum. Dyson called the conference "a meeting ground for the industry itself"[6] Most people just call it "Esther's." To get an invitation, you have to be a subscriber to *Release 1.0.* Still, there is not room for everyone who wants to attend. "The kind of people who come . . . don't need to make money—they already have it," someone said. "They simply want to solidify relationships with a select group of people."[7]

The conference, like the newsletter, is devoted to new ideas. In 1989, the Lotus software company showed its new product, Lotus Notes, at the conference. The public did not get to see Lotus Notes until nine months later. Esther Dyson has been surrounded by new ideas since she was born, on July 14, 1951. Her father, Freeman Dyson, is considered by some people to be the greatest living physicist.[8] Her mother, Verena Huber-Dyson, is a brilliant mathematician. When Esther and her brother, George, were growing up in Princeton, New Jersey, two of their neighbors were Nobel Prize winners. A third was the inventor of color television.

George Dyson thinks that having such brilliant parents made Esther determined to succeed. "My father is a hard act to follow," George Dyson said.[9] Esther Dyson was only fourteen when she began to study Russian. At age sixteen, she went to Radcliffe College. At that time, Radcliffe was a college for women only that was related to Harvard University. The men at Harvard who knew Dyson called her

"Tiny Esther."[10] At only five-feet-two-inches tall, she "really does resemble Peter Pan," one writer said.[11]

At Radcliffe, Dyson studied economics. She also worked as a reporter and copy editor for the Harvard *Crimson*, the university's newspaper. After she graduated in 1972, Dyson went to work for *Forbes*, an influential business magazine. Dyson called *Forbes* "a real-life business school: Instead of sitting in the library I got to go out and interview the principals who made everything happen."[12] Dyson was assigned to write stories about the brand-new computer companies that were just starting up.

After three years of writing about the business world, Dyson decided to become part of it. She went to work as a Wall Street analyst in 1977. Her job was "following high-tech stocks and trying to tell investors which companies would grow and prosper."[13] Since she knew about computer companies, they became her specialty. She researched Intel, Microsoft, and Apple when they were new.

Dyson discovered that she was less interested in the stock market than in the way companies worked and in the products they made. In 1982, she left Wall Street to learn more about the computer industry. She went to work for the *Rosen Electronics Newsletter*. Two years later, she bought the newsletter from its owner, Ben Rosen, and renamed it *Release 1.0*. Software companies call the very first version of their programs "release 1.0". Dyson's name for her newsletter stressed its emphasis on new ideas.

Dyson's newsletter, her conference, and various speaking engagements have made her a millionaire, but she does not spend much on herself. Most of the time, she wears blue jeans and T-shirts given to her by companies promoting their products. She has a small apartment in New York City that she bought twenty-five years ago. Dyson does not spend much time there. The apartment has no telephone. She does not have a car. In fact, she has never even had a driver's license.

Dyson uses her money—and her time—to invest in worthwhile projects. "Money enables me to invest in things I think should exist," she said.[14] For the past ten years, Dyson has been interested in Russia and Eastern Europe. The region is far behind the United States in technical development. Dyson acts as an "angel" for small Eastern European and Russian software and computer companies. She offers them advice on how to sell their products, reads their business plans and makes suggestions. When she thinks the companies are good investments, she finds wealthy investors in the United States. Sometimes she invests her own money in the companies.

Dyson also serves as the chairperson of the Electronic Frontiers Foundation (EFF). The organization focuses on the use of the Internet. Many people are concerned about the Internet, which gives everyone access to free information. For the most part, the information is good. But people can also learn to make bombs and other weapons. Some sites contain pornography, violence, and other content that people find offensive. There are groups who believe this content should be illegal. Dyson and EFF disagree. They believe that people must be taught to use the Internet responsibly. "This sounds really corny," she says, "but I simply hope to encourage more good people to get on the Net and not be scared. I want to invite nice new neighbors into my neighborhood."[15]

Dyson fears that any other action would limit free speech. It would restrict access to new ideas. And, of course, Esther Dyson believes in the value of new ideas. EFF is working to create guidelines for use of the Internet. "We're leading the fight for freedom of speech on the Net not just by arguing against censorship, but by promoting the notion that people should be able to control the content they (and their children) receive for themselves," Dyson wrote.[16]

Dyson is also the chairman of the board of directors of the Internet Corporation for Assigned Names and Numbers (ICANN). This nonprofit corporation helps to make the rules about the use of names and addresses on the Internet.

Because Dyson works so hard, she does not have much time for a personal life. She does not have pets. She has never been married. When Dyson was a little girl, she said she would only marry someone wealthier and smarter than she was. "When you're

Esther Dyson speaks at PC Forum, in Scottsdale, Arizona, one of the two annual conferences hosted by EDventures Holdings, Inc., of which she is president.

Esther, that limits the field," George Dyson said.[17] She has no children. "I believe in parents' being present for their children, and I did not want to be a bad mother," she said.[18]

In fact, Dyson does not seem to have close relationships with anyone. Her father said, "She doesn't need that. She never needed to come and talk about her problems, even when she was a child. . . . She was happy to be left alone. We hardly noticed her."[19]

Some people wonder whether Dyson had to work so hard because she is a woman. Was it harder for her to succeed? Dyson does not think so. "I was a girl, and there weren't many of them around in this business," recalls Dyson. "So maybe I became better known than I should be."[20]

Dyson does not follow anyone else's rules. In part, she says, that is easier for a woman to do in a man's world. In the computer world, successful men all compare themselves to Bill Gates. "Obviously, I've never had that problem," Dyson said.[21] Esther Dyson has no role models. That has made her free to create her own special role.

Steve Jobs

Chairman and CEO, Pixar Animation Studios; Cofounder and CEO, Apple Computer

On the morning after the 1984 Super Bowl, what many people talked about was not a touchdown, a pass, or a fumble. It was a television commercial. The commercial, which ran only one time, showed rows of dejected-looking men in drab uniforms, their heads shaved, sitting on benches facing a huge screen. From the screen, a stern-looking man—obviously the "Big Brother" of the novel *1984* by George Orwell—delivered an angry-sounding lecture. Suddenly, into the roomful of lifeless men a young woman athlete came running being chased by faceless storm troopers. She threw a sledgehammer at the screen, which shattered and burst into flames.

Steve Jobs

At the end of the commercial, an announcer's voice said, "On January 24, Apple Computer will introduce Macintosh. And you'll see why 1984 won't be like *1984*."[1]

The commercial announced an amazing development: A computer that could be operated by clicking on icons, or pictures, rather than typing in words. A graphical user interface makes it easy for anyone to own and operate a home computer.

"1984" was also a vivid sixty-second statement of what Steve Jobs, the cofounder of Apple Computer, has always believed: Computer technology is not just a product. It is, first and foremost, a way to change the world.

Steve Jobs is a child of the 1960s. He was born February 24, 1955, and was adopted as an infant by Paul and Clara Jobs. His parents, who later adopted a daughter, Patty, doted on their son. When Jobs announced that he would no longer attend an elementary school that he hated, the family moved from South San Francisco to Cupertino so their son could attend a different school.[2]

At Cupertino Junior High School, Jobs met Stephen Wozniak, known as "Woz." Wozniak was four years older than Jobs, already so absorbed in electronics that he did not have much of a social life. Through their similar interests, Jobs and Wozniak soon became best friends.

By the time Jobs reached high school, the counterculture movement was well under way in northern

California. Jobs read philosophy and literature as well as studying electronics. When he got his first car, he visited friends at Berkeley and Stanford. He experimented with drugs like marijuana, hashish, and LSD. He stopped eating meat and, at one point, tried a diet consisting of nothing but fruit.

When Jobs graduated from high school, he went to live with his girlfriend, Judy Smith, in a small cabin in the hills. But he discovered that, even for a free spirit, money was necessary. One of his part-time jobs was dressing up in an Alice in Wonderland costume at a shopping mall in San Jose. Jobs and Wozniak alternated as the White Rabbit and the Mad Hatter.

Steve Wozniak, who was a notorious practical joker, invented a "blue box" for making free long-distance phone calls. The box emitted a digital sound that precisely imitated the phone company's tone signals. For Woz, creating the blue box was a lark. But Steve Jobs quickly saw it as a moneymaking device. The two made a number of the blue boxes, which they sold for a total of six thousand dollars.[3] They gave up the business after narrowly avoiding being caught by the police with the illegal device.

After graduating from high school, Jobs attended Reed College in Portland, Oregon, for one semester. He enjoyed the college's liberal environment. He went barefoot and grew long hair and a beard. He joined a dance class, hoping to meet girls. Jobs seldom went to his other classes, but he enjoyed intense debates about the meaning of life. He became fascinated with Zen Buddhism, a religion.

After he dropped out of the college, Jobs stayed in Portland. At first, he lived in unused dormitory rooms on campus. Then he rented a room downtown for twenty-five dollars a month. He got a job as a maintenance man and continued to experiment with drugs. He wanted to make a pilgrimage to India to study Eastern religion. To raise the money for the trip, he moved home and found a job at Atari, a company that made video games.

Jobs managed to go to India for a prolonged visit in 1974. When he came back to California, he worked briefly for Atari once more. Then he headed for an Oregon commune called the All One Farm, where he worked picking apples.

After all this travel and experimenting with life, Jobs was still only twenty years old when he returned once again to Palo Alto in 1975. There, he discovered that Steve Wozniak had managed to design and build a working computer. Wozniak was giving away drawings of his computer design to members of the Homebrew Computer Club. As with the blue box, Jobs saw a way to make money from the invention. He suggested they form a computer company and call it "Apple," a reminder of the orchards at All One Farm. Jobs sold his Volkswagen van for $1,500 to help provide the money they needed for start-up.

While Wozniak was the computer's designer, Jobs was the "Scrambler."[4] He scrambled for bargain-priced parts. He scrambled for money. He scrambled for customers. Apple Computer set up shop in a spare bedroom of Paul and Clara Jobs' home. Steve Jobs's sister, Patty, assembled the circuit boards. Paul Jobs renovated the garage so the operation could expand. Clara Jobs took telephone messages.

From that start in 1977, Apple Computer grew rapidly. The Apple II was released in April 1978. It was, according to the ad copy, "a truly usable computer, the first for the masses." Thanks to Wozniak, it had color graphics. Jobs had designed an attractive plastic case. Apple sold more than $300 million worth of computers in its first five years in business. On December 12, 1980, Apple Computer went public, selling its shares on the stock market. By the end of the day, Steve Jobs, age twenty-five, was worth $256.4 million.

At work, Jobs could be stubborn. He insisted that he was right, against all the evidence to the contrary. Apple employees called this Jobs' "reality distortion field."[5] By 1982, Jobs had become obsessed with the idea that would become the Macintosh. He moved the Macintosh design team into a separate building, which flew a pirate flag from the roof. The Macintosh team treated other Apple employees with contempt—in spite of the fact that sales of the Apple II were what paid everyone's salaries.[6] Although the Macintosh was a success when it was launched in 1984, the company was divided. At a

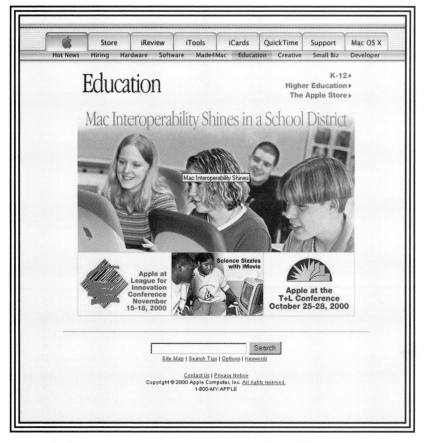

Apple Computer began in a spare bedroom of Steve Job's parents' house.

board meeting in April 1985, Steve Jobs was removed as head of the Macintosh division. In effect, the cofounder of Apple Computer no longer had a job with the company. In September 1985, Steve Jobs resigned.

That same year, Jobs started another computer company, NeXT, using $7 million of his own money. The NeXT computer would use a new technology called object-oriented programming. In February 1986, while the NeXT computer was still being developed, Jobs paid $10 million for a majority interest in Pixar Animation Studios. Pixar was the computer division of LucasFilm, Ltd., the company that had created *Star Wars* and other movies.

While NeXT progressed slowly, Pixar had a hit with its first movie, *Toy Story*, in 1995. *A Bug's Life*, released in 1998, was also a hit. This successful movie was followed by *Toy Story 2* in 1999.

Meanwhile, Apple Computer was going steadily downhill. Its new products never reached the popularity of the Macintosh. Its biggest competitor, the IBM PC, soon had its own user-friendly operating system, Microsoft Windows. Because PC computers had a different operating system from the Apple, most software would not work in both kinds of machines. Software companies had to choose one system or the other. Most of them decided to create software that was PC-compatible.

In December 1996, Apple announced its plans to buy NeXT. That move got Steve Jobs re-involved with the company he founded. On September 16, 1997, Apple Corporation appointed Steve Jobs as interim CEO.

In this position, Steve Jobs was paid one dollar a year. That salary was enough to qualify his family for the company health plan. Jobs owned only one share of Apple stock, so he could attend shareholders' meetings. Because he was not earning money from Apple, Jobs could do what he thought was right for the company. Nobody could accuse him of looking out only for himself.

In 1998, his first year as interim CEO, Jobs seemed to be doing things right. He pushed the company's iMac computer into the marketplace. The computer makes it easier for people to use the Internet. (That is what the letter i stands for.) It is also a cute, candy-colored computer that appeals to consumers. Apple sold 278,000 iMac computers in just six weeks.

Jobs also made a decision that some loyal Apple computer users found shocking: He sold seven percent of Apple Computer, Inc., to Microsoft Corporation. Jobs and his old rival, Bill Gates, are now colleagues. Microsoft now offers versions of its most popular software, including Microsoft Word, that are made for the Macintosh computer.

By accepting the deal with Microsoft, Jobs seemed to be announcing that Apple Computer would never again be the giant it once had been. Instead, the company will survive by developing in specialized areas. For example, Apple's new iMovie software is designed for editing film made with digital movie cameras.

The Steve Jobs who came back to Apple seems to have the old magic, but he also seems to be a new man. In 1991, he married Laurene Powell. Their son, Reed, was born that September. A daughter was born in August 1995. Jobs became a devoted family man, and his family grew to include his older daughter, Lisa. When he was in his thirties, Jobs finally met his birth mother. He also discovered that he had a half-sister, Mona Simpson, a novelist.

Regis McKenna, who created the earliest advertising campaigns for Apple, noticed the change. "He asked lots of people for advice when he returned to Apple and actually listened to them. He's learned from his mistakes."[7] In January 2000, Jobs accepted the chief executive officer position for the company he had helped to found.

Jobs had every reason to be pleased with his success. But the old arrogance seemed to be gone when he said, "Several months ago, I woke up and decided that . . . I will do as best as I can for as long as I can and not worry about what other people think. My focus is on my family, Apple, and Pixar, in that order."[8]

William H. Gates, III
Chair, Microsoft Corporation

Not many rummage sales change the world. But the one held by the Mothers Club at Lakeside School in Seattle in the late 1960s certainly did. The mothers used the money from the rummage sale to buy time on a mainframe computer and to install a terminal at the school so that the students could access the computer.

One of the mothers who helped with the sale was Mary Gates. Her son, Bill Gates, was one of the students who got to use the terminal at Lakeside School. In his book *The Road Ahead,* he called the investment in computer time a decision "I'll always be grateful for."[1]

The Lakeside Mothers Club thought the $3,000 they raised would last all year. Within weeks, it was

William H. Gates, III

gone. After that, the boys had to pay for the time themselves. "This is what drove me to the commercial side of the software business," Gates recalled. I needed money to buy access."[2]

Using what they had learned on the Lakeside school computer terminal, Bill and his friend Paul Allen were able to get entry-level jobs as software programmers. They could earn as much as five thousand dollars a summer—paid in a combination of cash and computer time. That was a lot of money for high school students in the 1960s.

In addition to earning spending money, Bill Gates found other ways to benefit from computers. He was asked to write the program for scheduling students into classes at Lakeside. By adding a few special instructions, Gates was able to make himself "nearly the only guy in a class full of girls."[3]

Around Lakeside School, Bill Gates was soon known as "the computer guy." Bill Gates does not really like that label. After all, computers were—and are—just one of his many interests. When he was eight years old, Gates decided to read the entire *World Book Encyclopedia*. He started with the first volume, "determined to read straight through every one."[4] He kept reading for five years and made it to the Ps.

Gates had a chance to catch up on his reading at the end of ninth grade. His parents were worried that he was becoming addicted to computers. For nine months, he gave up computing. He read biographies, business and science books, and novels. His favorite books were *Catcher in the Rye* by J. D. Salinger and *A Separate Peace: A Novel* by John Knowles.[5]

Born on October 28, 1955, Gates and his two sisters grew up in Seattle, Washington. Their father, William H. Gates II, was a Seattle lawyer. Their mother, Mary Gates, was a schoolteacher, University of Washington regent and chairwoman of the United Way.

Bill Gates was "a good rollerskater, a decent tennis player, a straight, fast, formless, reckless snow skier, and . . . a passionate, stylish waterskier."[6] He became a Boy Scout and came within two or three merit badges of making Eagle Scout. He even had leading roles in two school plays. For one of them, he had to memorize a three-page monologue. He did it in minutes, just by glancing through the pages.

When Gates enrolled at Harvard University in 1973, his first major was economics. Then he switched to mathematics. He thought about switching again, to psychology, or maybe preparing for law school. He admits, though, that he spent a lot of time playing poker. These were serious games, where it was possible to lose two thousand dollars in a session. Playing poker taught him a lot about strategy—lessons that he would use in the business world.[7]

Bill Gates kept in touch with his friend Paul Allen. The two were already wondering if they could form a company to make software. Then, in

December 1974, Allen showed Gates a copy of the January issue of *Popular Electronics*. On the cover of the magazine was "a photograph of a very small computer, not much larger than a toaster oven."[8] Called the Altair 8800, the little computer had an Intel 8080 microprocessor chip as its brain. MITS, the company that invented the Altair 8800, was selling it as a kit for less than four hundred dollars.

Gates and Allen knew that the Altair was the start of the computer revolution. It was a computer that people could write "real" software for. "The future was staring us in the face from the cover of a magazine. It was not going to wait for us," Gates recalled.[9]

Gates and Allen started by writing a version of the programming language BASIC for the Altair. It took five weeks during the winter of 1975. Gates "lost track of night and day." When he slept at all, it was at his desk or on the floor. Some days he forgot to eat.[10] When they were finished, they took their program to Albuquerque, New Mexico, and showed it to the people at MITS. MITS liked the program. They offered to pay Gates and Allen royalties for using the program in the Altair.

Gates took a leave of absence from Harvard so that he and Paul Allen could start their software company. To fund the company, Gates invested the money he had won in his college poker games. Gates and Allen moved their little software company, which they called Microsoft, home to Seattle.

By 1977, other companies were making personal computers. Microsoft expanded by creating versions of BASIC for these companies: Apple, Commodore, Radio Shack, and Texas Instruments. Bill Gates was the Microsoft salesman in those years. "I was barely out of my teens, and selling intimidated me," he recalled.[11] The company's strategy was to charge the company that made the computer a licensing fee. That gave the company the right to sell Microsoft software along with its computers. Gates and Allen had tried selling Altair BASIC to computer users, but the users often copied each others' software, without paying the inventor for it.

When IBM entered the personal computer business in 1980, they chose Microsoft, too. Soon, the "PCdos" operating system that Microsoft had devised for IBM had become the industry standard. Microsoft grew quickly by developing other applications, like Microsoft Word, to run on its operating system.

While Microsoft was growing, Bill Gates was growing up. He was barely out of his teens when Microsoft was founded. One day, a new Microsoft secretary became alarmed when a "kid" walked past her desk and into Bill Gates' office. She was amazed to be told that the kid *was* Bill Gates.[12] In many ways, he still acted like a kid. Gates loved fast cars. One story about him says that he got three speeding tickets on his drive from Albuquerque back home to Seattle—two of them from the same policeman, both for going 110 miles an hour.[13] But Gates was also famous for being absentminded. He ruined the motor of his expensive Porsche sports car by forgetting to put oil in it.

Bill Gates may have been young and eccentric, but he was also a competitive businessman. He had grown up in a family that had jigsaw puzzle competitions and where the children would play cards to decide who had to wash dishes. He was shy, but he pushed himself and everyone else very hard.

One of the things he pushed for was a "graphical user interface" for the personal computer. The Apple MacIntosh had already introduced such a system, which let users click on pictures, or icons, instead of typing in words to tell the computer what to do. In 1984, Microsoft introduced Windows. It was the "killer app" that made Microsoft a giant company and made Bill Gates the richest man in the world.

But he was not content. By the mid-1990s, Gates saw the importance of the Internet. He developed an application called Microsoft Windows Explorer to help people navigate the Internet. He wrote a book called *Business @ the Speed of Thought* about how the Internet would shape the future.

On New Year's Day, 1994, Bill Gates married Melinda French, a Microsoft executive. They built a house on Lake Washington, near Seattle, that cost an estimated $75 million. It has an underground garage for 100 cars. "I still can't enjoy these things without

Microsoft has continued to grow under Bill Gates's guidance.

feeling a little guilty about it," Gates says.[14] Bill and Melinda Gates have two children. Their daughter, Jennifer Katharine Gates, was born in 1996. Their son, Rory John Gates, was born in 1999.

In 1994, Mary Gates died of breast cancer. She had devoted her life to charities like the United Way. Since her death, Bill Gates has become interested in giving away a large part of his fortune. He has given more than $17 billion to the William H. Gates Foundation. Supervised by his father, Bill Gates, Sr., the foundation contributes to education and global health. It also supports community projects in the Pacific Northwest. "As far as I can tell," Bill Gates, Sr., said, "I'm the only dad who's been charged with the task of giving away his son's money."[15]

During the 1990s, the size and wealth of Microsoft made Bill Gates a target of criticism. The Department of Justice investigated Microsoft's policy of charging companies a royalty on every computer they made, whether they installed Microsoft products or not. That was unfair competition, the Department of Justice said. Microsoft changed the practice.

In 1997, the Department of Justice brought a new charge against Microsoft. By bundling its Microsoft Internet Explorer with other Windows software, Microsoft has made it hard for other Internet software companies, like Netscape, to compete, the Department of Justice said.

On June 7, 2000, Federal Judge Thomas Penfield Jackson ruled that Microsoft's business practices were "predatory" and unfair to competition. He ordered that Microsoft be split into two companies. One company would continue to make and sell operating systems like Windows 98, Windows 2000, and Windows NT. The other would market Microsoft's other software, including the Microsoft Internet Explorer Internet browser.

"I think this ruling flies in the face of what consumers experience every day—a high-tech economy that's lowering prices and bringing out lots of great new products," Bill Gates said. He called Judge Turner's ruling unfair to Microsoft. "It's not just the breakup, but also the fact that when we do innovative work we have to give it to our competitors, rather than get the benefits of our innovation."[16]

Microsoft immediately appealed the ruling. Most people agree that the case will eventually be heard by the United States Supreme Court. But how the decision will affect Microsoft, and Bill Gates, is open to debate. Some people think that, no matter what the outcome, Microsoft will be damaged. Too much of the company's time and energy is being spent on the court case, which takes away from its ability to innovate and compete. Others think a divided Microsoft will simply become twice as strong.

There is no doubt that the world's richest man is facing his toughest challenge yet.

Steve Case

Founder, America Online

Steve Case, the founder of America Online, learned about the Internet while eating pizza. In the early 1980s, eating pizza was his job, and using the Internet was just a hobby. Steve Case worked for Pizza Hut as a manager of new pizza development. To find new ingredients for pizza, Case traveled around the country. In every town and city, he went to the best-known pizza restaurant and ordered its most popular kind of pizza.

That might sound like an exciting job. But being on the road all alone, month after month, got boring. Case bought a portable computer to take along. Back then, "portable" meant the size and weight of a heavy suitcase. From his hotel, Case would connect

Steve Case

the computer to his phone line with a modem and dial up computer bulletin boards and chat lines. The computer gave him a way to pass the time. The messages to and from people around the country made him feel less lonely. "There was something magical about the notion of sitting in Wichita and talking to the world," Case recalled.[1]

What Steve Case learned about pizzas and the Internet would be very useful when he had his own company. Nobody expected him to work for Pizza Hut forever. "He's always been an independent thinker," his older brother, Dan, explained.[2]

Case comes from a family of ambitious and competitive businesspeople. He was born August 21, 1958 and raised in Honolulu, Hawaii. His father was a successful attorney. His mother was a schoolteacher. Steve Case is the third of four children. His sister Carin was oldest and his brother Jeff was youngest. In between were Steve and Dan, just thirteen months apart and very close friends. When Steve Case was six years old, the two brothers started a juice stand. They used fruit from the trees in their backyard, which kept their costs low. The brothers charged two cents for a glass of juice. Most people gave them a nickel and told them to keep the change, which provided a lot of profit.

As teenagers, the brothers started a company called Case Enterprises. They sold seeds from door to door and delivered newspapers. They started another company, Aloha Sales Agency, to publish an advertising circular called "Budget Booster."[3]

In high school, Case found a way to get free record albums. First, he volunteered to write album reviews for his school newspaper. Then, he wrote to some small record companies and told them that he was the music critic for Hawaii's largest student newspaper. The companies sent him free albums to review. Case wrote some reviews. When they were published, he sent them to the big record companies. Soon, those companies were also sending him records. He got free concert tickets, too.

Case's interest in music continued when he went to Williams College, in Massachusetts. Although it was far from his home in Hawaii, Williams College was where his father had attended school. Case majored in political science and, in his spare time, put on rock concerts. He also sang with two rock and roll bands. Case was not a very good singer. "Since I did not have a voice, I had to compensate with stage presence," he later told a reporter.[4]

Case graduated from college in 1980. He took a job with Proctor & Gamble in their marketing department. First, Case worked with the Lilt home permanent kit. It was an old-fashioned product that Case tried to make popular again. Then he got another assignment. Proctor & Gamble had introduced fabric softener sheets to be used in clothes dryers. Since the product was very popular, the company decided the same idea would work for hair conditioner. They called it a "wipe-on" hair conditioner. Case was supposed to figure out how to sell the product. The slogan for the product was "Towelette? You bet!"[5] The product failed miserably.

In 1982, Case left Proctor & Gamble for PepsiCo. He was assigned to Pizza Hut, a company owned by PepsiCo. That is when he traveled the country, tasting pizzas and playing with computer bulletin boards and chat lines.

Then, in 1983, Case went to a consumer electronics show with his brother Dan. By then, Dan Case had become an investment banker. Dan's company loaned money to new companies to start their businesses. One of those companies, Control Video Corporation, delivered Atari video games via modem to personal computers. Dan Case thought that his brother could help the new company with its marketing.

Steve Case left PepsiCo for Control Video. Almost immediately, the new company started to collapse. Atari video games had become less popular. The new company did not have enough money. The company's board of directors fired nearly all of its managers and hired a new CEO named Jim Kimsey. Steve Case was the only person in the marketing department who was not fired. "Steve was promoted to VP of marketing because there was no one else left," his brother Dan said.[6] In 1985, Kimsey and Case set out to rebuild the company.

Case helped to bring in more money from investors to keep the company going. Then he and Kimsey came up with new services the company could sell. They developed services that could be offered "online," that is, delivered via modem. But the services were for computer users, not video game players.

The company was now called Quantum Computer Services. Case used the same approach that had worked with the record companies. First, the company got some subscribers for its services. Those users owned an inexpensive home computer called the Commodore. Then, Case went to Apple Computer. He showed what his company had done for Commodore. He made an arrangement to provide special services to Apple Computer users. He used that success to make a deal with IBM. At the time, IBM was the biggest computer company.

In 1991, Jim Kimsey moved up from chief executive officer to chairman of the board at Quantum Computer Services. He named Steve Case the CEO. The next year, 1992, Quantum was renamed America Online.

At that time, some other companies were already offering online services. CompuServe was owned by H&R Block. Prodigy was a joint venture of IBM and Sears. It seemed impossible for the little start-up company to stand up to those giants. Even Case's mother was worried. Could her son's company actually compete with Sears?[7]

But Steve Case had learned a lot from working for Proctor & Gamble and Pizza Hut. He knew that consumers liked things simple. New technology, like hair conditioner towelettes, did not always appeal to them. Most of the time, exotic toppings on pizza were not as popular as cheese and pepperoni. Steve Case knew that customers would feel the same way about online computer services. A *Time* magazine article explained that AOL succeeded because Steve Case made the Internet easy to use. Case thinks that only a small number of "geeks" really want complicated technology. "Our market is everyone else," he told a reporter.[8]

Steve Case seems to live his "keep it simple" philosophy. He dresses casually, in khaki pants and plaid shirts. He talks quietly, often putting his feet up on his desk.[9]

America Online grew very fast because it offered what customers wanted. AOL, as it called, had 600,000 subscribers in early 1994. A year later, membership passed 2 million. By August 1996, AOL had 6.3 million subscribers. That made the company the leading provider of online services, and it has been the leader ever since.

But the fast growth caused problems. In the winter of 1993–1994, the number of customers had grown too fast for AOL's hardware. When subscribers tried to dial up, they got busy signals. Even if they got through to AOL, the service would run

According to Case, the future is online.

very slowly. Critics started calling the company "America On Hold."[10]

Adding new hardware would cost AOL a lot of money and would take some time. In February 1994, the company asked its subscribers to use its services less. This angered many customers, who thought AOL wanted to provide less service while charging the same amount of money.

Steve Case continued to work hard to meet his customers' needs. AOL added capacity. The company delayed some new services that might have caused problems. The company continued to grow, but problems continued, too. In the summer of 1996, AOL had a 19-hour outage, when customers could not get through at all.

Adding capacity to service its customers is costly for AOL. For example, in 1995 the company's revenues were $394 million. But AOL still lost $33 million that year because it had to spend so much on new hardware and hiring new employees.

AOL's fast growth may have been costly to Steve Case's personal life, too. In 1996, he separated from his wife, Joanne. They had met at college, married in 1985, and had three children. Shortly after his separation, Case announced that he was dating a top-ranking AOL executive, Jean Villaneuva.

Through it all, AOL continued to grow, and the value of its stock continued to increase, providing the company with money it needs for growth.

In January 2001, AOL merged with Time Warner, creating a single company with an estimated value of $181.9 billion. The merger gives AOL access to cable television companies that may someday provide Internet service. Time Warner's many magazines and publishing companies give AOL access to content for the Internet. As head of AOL Time Warner, Inc., Steve Case remains true to his business philosophy: Stay in touch with the consumer. He hopes to find even more ways to give consumers what they want.

8

Jeffrey P. Bezos
Founder and CEO, Amazon

When Jeff Bezos was three years old, he told his parents that he was tired of sleeping in a crib. He wanted a real bed. His mother told him he would have to wait awhile. But Jeff Bezos does not like to wait. When his mother came home, she found him trying to disassemble his crib with a screwdriver. "It was always hard to stay a step ahead of him," Jackie Bezos recalls.[1]

As the founder of Amazon, Jeff Bezos is still doing what he wants to do, sometimes against the advice of his friends and business experts. In its first three years of business, Amazon.com became the third-largest bookseller in the world. In those three years, Amazon achieved $150 million in sales. The company's sales after three years in business were as

Jeffrey P. Bezos

large as Wal-Mart's sales after twelve years.[2] But the company has never made a profit, and some critics say that it never will.

Bezos, the oldest of three children, is the son of an immigrant from Cuba who became a successful petroleum engineer. Jeff Bezos was born on January 12, 1964. He grew up in Miami and Houston and also spent a lot of time on his grandfather's Texas ranch. He had an active boyhood. He owned a pet raccoon named Ringo. By the time he was sixteen, he recalled later, "I could fix windmills, use an arc welder and castrate cattle."[3]

But Bezos also paid attention to his studies and was able to get into Princeton University. He majored in electrical engineering and computer science, graduating summa cum laude (with highest honors) in 1986.[4] After college, Bezos joined the business world. He worked for a new company called FITEL for two years. The company developed software that tracked international stock trades.[5] That experience helped Bezos learn about the financial industry. In 1988, he took a job at Bankers Trust Company in New York. Using his computer science background, Bezos helped the company develop computer systems to manage investors' money. Bezos became the company's youngest vice president in February 1990. By that time, he was helping to manage more than $250 billion in assets.

Bezos went to work for another investment company, D.E. Shaw & Co. As he had at Bankers Trust, Bezos helped his new company develop high-tech systems to manage investments. Bezos was so good at his job that he became the company's youngest senior vice president in 1992.[6]

Bezos seemed to be on a fast track to success in New York. In the companies he worked for, Bezos was on the leading edge of technology, but he was not satisfied.

As a boy, Jeff Bezos had wanted to be an astronaut, and as an adult, he wanted to reach for the stars. In 1994, Bezos read that usage of the World Wide Web was growing by 2,300 percent a year.[7] The Internet seemed like the "final frontier," and Bezos wanted to go exploring.

Starting with the idea that he wanted to launch an Internet company, Bezos thought logically about what kind of company it should be. As Jerry Yang, the founder of Yahoo, was discovering at about the same time, it is hard to make a profit from the content of a website. Bezos decided his business would make money through transactions. He also decided that "vertical industry groups were a good place to start."[8] In other words, he wanted his website to specialize in a single category of product, but one that would appeal to a wide range of buyers.

Bezos made a list of twenty possibilities and ranked them according to their moneymaking potential. The top four options were books, software, music, and videos.[9] Bezos decided to start his business by selling books because "books have a very unusual characteristic; there are so many different books. That's totally different from any other product category."[10] No bookstore could make room for 1.5 million books, but that is how many titles there are in print at any one time, just in English![11] For an Internet company, space was not a problem. The books would be stored by publishers and distributors around the country until the customer ordered them.

Although Bezos was living in New York, he knew that was not the right place to start his company. He needed an area with many high-tech businesses, so he could find employees to help him develop his company. Although he wanted lots of available employees, he still wanted a state with a small population. That way, few of the customer orders would come from in-state, and he would not have to collect and pay as much state sales tax. Seattle, Washington, the home of Microsoft, seemed like a logical place for his company to start.[12]

Now that he knew what his company would do, and where it would be located, Jeff Bezos had to figure out what it would be called. He wanted the name to start with the letter A, so it would always be listed first in alphabetical order. He wanted something that would be easy to spell. Since the Internet is a worldwide medium, he wanted a name that would be

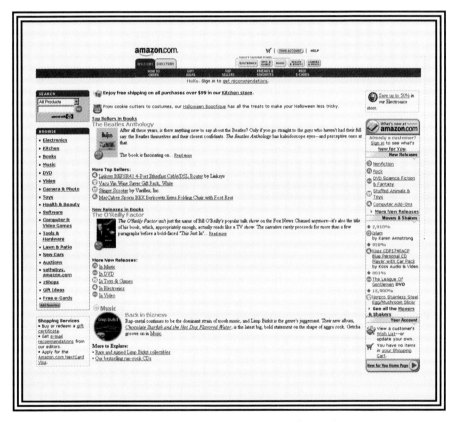

Amazon.com is the company Bezos founded.

recognizable anywhere in the world. And, since he intended to create a big company, he wanted a name that sounded big. "Earth's biggest river, Earth's biggest bookstore," Bezos explained. "The Amazon River is 10 times as large as the next largest river, which is the Mississippi, in terms of volume of water. Twenty percent of the world's fresh water is in the Amazon River Basin, and we have six times as many titles as the world's largest physical bookstore."[13]

Bezos knew he had a good idea. And in 1995, with nothing more than an idea, he quit his high-paying job in New York City. He and his wife drove across the country to Seattle. The company started in the garage of his rented house. He bought four doors at a lumberyard, and put four-by-fours on the corners for legs. Those were the first desks at Amazon.[14] In 1998, one of those desks sold in an Amazon charity auction for $30,100![15]

"We spend money on the things that matter to our customers," Bezos says, "and we don't spend money on anything else."[16] Bezos even used a stack of old phone books as a monitor stand.[17] Bezos was careful with money because he was not sure his new company would succeed. He told an interviewer, "The odds-on bet was that it wouldn't work. I told all of our original investors that they would lose their money for sure."[18]

Those investors have grown rich because the company's stock is worth as much as $30 billion.[19] Bezos has found more and more "vertical industries" to grow into, but he insists that "we're not a book company. We're not a music company. We're not a video company. We're not an auctions company. We're a customer company."[20]

But Amazon has never earned a profit. The bigger the company grows, the more it loses. At that rate, it will be harder and harder for Jeffrey Bezos to keep moving ahead.

Jerry Yang
Founder, Yahoo

The title on Jerry Yang's business card reads "Chief Yahoo." That is just one sign that Yahoo is not a typical company. And Jerry Yang, who founded the company with David Filo, is not a typical businessman. His company, and his success, happened almost by accident.

Jerry Yang was born Chi-Yuan Yang in Taiwan on November 6, 1968. His mother, Lily, remembers the young Chi-Yuan as "irritatingly precocious." "Ever since he started to speak," she says, "he was very annoying, always asking, 'What is this?' 'Why?' He started to learn Chinese characters at three."[1]

When Chi-Yuan Yang was two years old, his father died. When he was nine, his mother brought him and his younger brother to the United States.

Jerry Yang

The two boys took the Americanized names "Jerry" and "Ken." The family settled in San Jose, California, and Lily worked as a maid.

Yang spoke very little English when he came to the United States. He still switches easily to Mandarin Chinese when he speaks to his mother on the telephone. But he soon became a straight A student. By 1990, he had earned bachelor's and master's degrees in electrical engineering from Stanford University, in Stanford, California. Since there were not many jobs for electrical engineers at the time, Yang decided to say in school. He enrolled in Stanford's doctoral program.

Yang was assigned to share an office in a trailer with David Filo, who had grown up in a commune in Moss Bluff, Louisiana. Yang and Filo were supposed to do research on computer-aided circuit design. But their advisor was on sabbatical, away from the university, doing his own research. With no one around to advise them, Yang and Filo did not get much work done. "I was quasi-retired at 23, playing a lot of golf," Yang recalls.[2]

They also used their office computers to explore the Internet. Getting around was not easy. Every site on the Internet has an address, called a URL, or "uniform resource locator." The only way to get to the site is by using the URL. In 1990, when Yang started using the Internet, there was no central directory. Imagine trying to call someone in a distant city without having a phone book or even an operator to ask for the number. That is what it was like to use the Internet.

Some of Yang's favorite sites were devoted to sumo wrestling. He put links to those sites on his own home page on the Internet. The Jerry Yang home page showed a picture of himself, holding a scorecard from Stanford's golf course. It also carried Jerry Yang's real name, in Chinese characters.

Yang kept track of other interesting URLs he found during his research. He put the list onto Stanford's computer system. The list was called "Jerry's Guide to the World Wide Web." Later David Filo added his favorite URLs. Then the list was called "Jerry and David's Guide to the World Wide Web." The list included categories like "Hard to Believe" and "Cool Links."

The list became very popular. Before long, the two students were spending all of their time updating it. In addition, they had to design the software for their directory. The software had to accept more and more entries. They spent so much time in their trailer-office that they kept a sleeping bag in the corner. Obviously, they were not getting much of their doctoral research done.

By 1994, Jerry and David had to make a decision. Should they finish their doctoral work? Or should they work full-time on their Internet directory? They were only three months from finishing school. Still, the decision was not hard. "We weren't academics," Jerry Yang told a reporter. "We could finish our Ph.D.s anytime, but entrepreneurial opportunity knocks only so often."[3]

A real business needed a real name. Jerry and David thought about a lot of names. Finally, they came up with Yahoo. According to Jerry Yang, "The date is hazy, but it was definitely at two A.M."[4] The name stands for "Yet Another Hierarchic Officious Oracle." The name was an inside joke. Computer people knew about another program, YACC. Its name stood for "Yet Another Compiler Compiler."

Yahoo has another meaning. The yahoos are characters in a book called *Gulliver's Travels*. They are rude people with no manners. The stereotype of today's computer "geek" is a modern-day yahoo. Jerry Yang was poking fun at people who spent all their time on the Internet. Of course, he was one of those people!

When Jerry and David decided not to finish their degrees, they had to leave their office at Stanford. They needed to rent office space and buy their own computers. Several people offered to invest in their company. Steve Case, the founder of America Online, wanted to buy Yahoo and make it part of his company. Microsoft wanted a partnership with Yahoo. Yang and Filo turned those offers down. They did not care about money. They wanted to keep their company, but Yahoo still had a long way to go.

Finally, a company called Sequoia Capital lent a million dollars to Yahoo. The founders were able to rent offices and buy computers. They hired some of their friends to work for the company. Jerry and David also did a very smart thing. They hired Tim Koogle to be the chief executive officer of the company. They did not want to think like businesspeople, but they knew somebody had to. A reporter said that the CEO is "probably the only person on the staff who owns both a tie and a pair of hard-soled shoes."[5]

With Tim Koogle as CEO, Yang and Filo were free to be "Chief Yahoos." Jerry Yang said about David Filo, "There was hardly ever any tension between him and I. It's just a fantastic relationship, and I hope it's a lifelong one."[6]

Jerry Yang is more outgoing than his partner. He became the public spokesperson for the company. Jerry bought a truck and a cell phone. But he was far from rich. So far, there was no way for Yahoo to make money. Anyone could use the directory for free.

To make Yahoo a paying business, Yang and Filo decided to sell advertising. That was a controversial decision. The Internet was started by the government. Most of its users at that time were in government or universities. Many people thought that making money from the Internet was wrong. Still, the company needed money, and the founders of Yahoo did not want to charge people for using the directory. In August of 1995, Yahoo sold advertising to five businesses. It charged them $60,000 apiece for a three-month trial. Some users accused Yahoo of

According to Yang, "The level at which people are building up connectivity [on the World Wide Web] is growing by leaps and bounds."

selling out.[7] Before long, however, other companies were selling advertising, too. By 1996, 350 companies advertised on Yahoo.

On April 12, 1996, Yahoo became a public company. Shares of the company's stock were sold to investors. In one day, the price of the stock went from $13 to $43. At the end of the day, the stock was worth $33 a share. Jerry Yang made $132 million that day. Yang told a reporter the success has not changed him, "except that I think more about taxes."[8]

Yang has much less time to play golf than he had as a graduate student. He bought a house, and in 1997 he married his longtime girlfriend, Akiko. (Akiko does not wish to have her maiden name appear.) His wife complains, "It's all work and no play."[9] Yang, who is still one of the youngest of the cyber elite, jokes, "I'm getting too old for this business.

But things are not likely to slow down anytime soon. Yahoo now draws more than 36 million visitors to its Web site each month. Because it also has nearly four thousand advertisers, the company actually makes a profit—a rare thing in Internet businesses! Like other Internet businesses, Yahoo is looking for ways to expand. It has purchased Geocities, a company that hosts personal Web pages. Yahoo plans to help Kmart launch an online store. The company will also be offering its services through mobile computer devices like cellular telephones.

Jerry Yang thinks that is just "the tip of the iceberg." "The level at which people are building up connectivity is growing by leaps and bounds," he says. "As a commercial medium, the Net hasn't yet been tapped."[10]

Linus Torvalds

Linus Torvalds
Developer of Linux

Who is the most popular man in Finland? If you judge by the number of listings on the Internet, it is not a famous hockey player, a rock musician, or even the prime minister. It is Linus Torvalds, a computer programmer. Linux, a software program he started writing in college, has made Linus Torvalds a hero to computer users around the world.

Born in Helsinki, Finland, on December 28, 1969, Linus Torvalds got hooked on computers when he was ten years old. His grandfather, a mathematician, bought a Commodore computer in 1980. Torvalds, who did not like playing hockey, became his grandfather's "right-hand man." Soon, he was writing his own computer games.

The Commodore computer was not very powerful, and soon it was obsolete. Torvalds got a British computer called a Sinclair QL, which was not compatible with many software programs. He learned to write his own software.

In 1988, Torvalds went to the University of Helsinki to study computer programming. The University's computers used an operating system called Unix. It was powerful, and it was stable. A computer using Unix could run for days or weeks without freezing or crashing. That was important for doing long calculations or running complex computer programs.

When Torvalds finally bought his own computer, in 1990, he wanted an operating system as powerful and stable as Unix. "I knew I did not want to use DOS," he said. "I'd seen DOS." But a basic Unix system cost $5,000—too much for a university student.[1]

Linus Torvalds did for his PC what he had done for his Sinclair QL: He started writing his own computer programming code. "Forget about dating! Forget about hobbies! Forget about life!" he says. "We are talking about a guy who sat, ate and slept in front of the computer."[2] At first, he wrote specific programs to handle certain computer tasks. But after he had written several programs, he realized that they added up to a basic operating system. Torvalds named his operating system Linux, a combination of his own first name and Unix, the operating system he could not afford to buy.[3]

In 1991, Torvalds decided to show Linux to some other people. He posted it on the Internet and shared it with friends. He said later, "making it available was mostly a 'look at what I've done—isn't this neat?' kind of thing. Hoping it would be useful to somebody, but certainly there is some element of 'showing off' in there too."[4]

"The first thing I got was a lot of comments," Torvalds recalls. Some people suggested improvements and additions to Linux. But other people actually made the improvements themselves and sent Torvalds their new code. "It got better and better" with other people's contributions, Torvalds says.[5]

Torvalds copyrighted the Linux system. He even created a Linux mascot, a penguin. He used the penguin mascot "partly because I like penguins. Partly because I was bitten by a penguin. It was at an open zoo. I made my finger look like a herring—and the penguin fell for it. It was a very timid bite."[6]

The initial copyright for Linux was "pretty strict," according to Torvalds. It said that nobody could distribute Linux for money. Anybody making changes to the code had to send the changes to Torvalds, so that he could use them later if he wanted to.[7]

But, with so many people wanting to work on Linux, the copyright rules got in the way. People could not even copy the system onto disks for friends, because they could not charge for the disks. Torvalds decided to change the Linux copyright to a "copyleft"—a public license that let anyone use Linux. Anyone can make a copy of Linux software from a friend's system or from the Internet. Companies can even make money by selling copies of the software. But everyone has to share the programming instructions, or source code. If anyone makes improvements to the code, they have to share those improvements, too.

Linus Torvalds believes that public licensing is the best way to create reliable software. He says, "everybody puts in effort into making Linux better, and everybody gets everybody else's effort back . . . Imagine ten people putting in one hour each every day on the project. They put in one hour of work, but because they share the end results they get nine hours of 'other people's work' for free."[8]

Soon, thousands of programmers around the world were working on Linux. All of the changes had to come back to Torvalds, who decides which changes to add to the system. Until 1997, Torvalds was still officially working for Helsinki University in Helsinki, Finland as a researcher. The University let Torvalds do his research on Linux. His University salary was the only money he made from Linux. Some of the users of Linux chipped in to help Torvalds pay for the computer he was using for Linux development. He also got some free

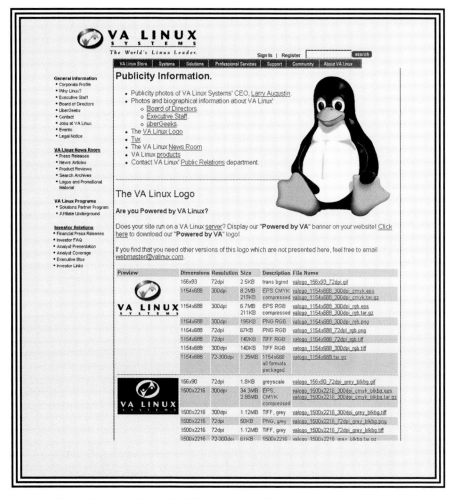

Torvalds copyrighted his Linux system. He even created a Linux mascot, a penguin.

"vacations" when computer groups paid him to come and give speeches about Linux.

By publicly licensing Linux, Torvalds was giving up the chance to get rich. But he does not seem to mind. When someone asked him if he had ever figured out how much money he would have made by licensing Linux, he replied, "I haven't even tried. I know how much fun I've had."[9]

"Making Linux freely available is the single best decision I've ever made," he said. The people who use Linux have helped to build the system. "I simply had no idea what features people would want to have, and if I had continued to do Linux on my own it would have been a much less interesting and complete system."[10]

Torvalds also knew that developing Linux was only the beginning of his career. "I don't expect to go hungry if I decide to leave the University. 'Resume: Linux' looks pretty good in many places," he told an interviewer.[11]

Indeed, Torvalds did leave Helsinki University in 1997. He and his wife, Tove, moved to California's Silicon Valley. He took a job with a new company called Transmeta. The company allows Torvalds to continue to work on Linux as part of his job. In May 2000, America Online (AOL) and Gateway Computer Company announced that they would develop a new "Internet appliance" that would use the Linux operating system and a microprocessor designed by Transmeta.

Although Linus Torvalds is a hero to thousands of Linux users, he has some critics, too. They say he holds too much control over Linux development. When his two daughters were born—Patricia Miranda in 1996 and Daniela in 1998—development of Linux slowed down. Later that year, he took a vacation from Linux, and some people wondered whether he was tired of the huge responsibility. In August 1999, Red Hat, one of the companies that distributes Linux for profit, became a publicly traded company. Now that some people can get rich by selling Linux, many of the volunteer developers will probably stop working on it.[12]

If commercial companies do take over the development of Linux, Torvalds will probably find other things to do. He likes to read. He says, "I read anything, mostly trash, science fiction, mystery thrillers, fantasy, detective stories." He likes to play billiards. And, after all, when he is asked about his greatest accomplishment, it is not Linux he mentions. Instead, it is "My life, being married with two children."[13]

Chapter Notes

Chapter 1. Andrew Grove

1. Brent Schlender, "The Incredible, Profitable Career of Andy Grove," *Fortune*, v. 137, n. 8, April 27, 1998, p. 34.

2. Joshua Cooper Ramo, "A Survivor's Tale," *Time*, December 29, 1997, pp. 54–63.

3. "The Boss," *Worth Online*, November, 1997, <http://www.worth.com/articles/Z9711C09.html> (June 14, 2000).

4. Tim Jackson, *Inside Intel: Andy Grove and the Rise of the World's Most Powerful Chip Company* (New York: Dutton, 1997), p. 67.

5. Ibid., p. 67.

6. Ibid., p. 253.

7. Andrew Grove, "My Biggest Mistake," *Inc.*, May 1998, p. 117.

8. Andrew Grove, "Taking on Prostate Cancer," *Fortune*, May 13, 1996, p. 60.

9. Ibid., p. 72.

10. Schlender, p. 35.

11. Ramo, p. 58.

12. "A Conversation with Andy Grove," *Fortune*, July 7, 1997, p. 186.

Chapter 2. Lawrence Ellison

1. Mike Wilson, *The Difference Between God and Larry Ellison: Inside Oracle Corporation* (New York: William Morrow and Company, Inc., 1997), p. 312.

2. Ibid., p. 18.

3. *Oral and Video Histories*, October 24, 1995, <http://www.si.edu/resource/tours/comphist/le1.html> (June 20, 2000).

4. Wilson, p. 27.

5. Wilson.

6. Wilson, p. 33.

7. Ibid., pp. 37–38.

8. Ibid., p. 99.

9. Ibid., p. 160.

10. Ibid., p. 13.

11. Janice Maloney, "Larry Ellison Is Captain Ahab and Bill Gates Is Moby Dick," *Fortune*, October 28, 1996, <http://www.fortune.com/fortune/1996/961028/orc.html> (June 20, 2000).

12. "Herring Top 100 Companies," *Red Herring*, June, 2000, <http://www.redherring.com/mag/issue79/herring100/oracle.html> (June 20, 2000).

13. Joshua Cooper Ramo and David S. Jackson, "The Prince of San Mateo," *Time*, May 12, 1997, pp. 58–60.

14. Maloney.

Chapter 3. Ann Winblad

1. Jill Wolfson and Carla Sequeiros, "The Revolutionaries: Ann Winblad," The Tech Museum of Innovation, n.d. <http://www.thetech.org/exhibits_events/online/revolution/winblad> (June 13, 2000).

2. Ibid.

3. Ibid.

4. Ibid.

5. Soledad O'Brien, "Spotlight Interview: Ann Winblad," Women.com, n.d., <http://women.com/tech/spotlight/winblad.html> (June 13, 2000).

6. Ibid.

7. Wolfson and Sequeiros.

8. David Diamond, "Adventure Capitalist," *Wired Magazine*, September, 1996, <http://www.wired.com/wired/archive/4.09/winblad.html> (June 22, 2000)

9. O'Brien.

10. "Venture Capital: Ann Winblad," *New Media News Special*, <http://www.newsmedianews.com/032197/wit_vc.html> (June 23, 2000).

11. Ann Winblad, "Coaching in the Software Industry Playoffs," *Red Herring Magazine*, September, 1997, <http://www.redherring.com/mag/issue46/ann/html> (November 20, 2000).

12. Andrew Serwer and Roberta Kirwan, "The Techie," *Money*, October 1998, pages 119–120.

13. New Media News Special.

14. Wolfson and Sequeiros.

Chapter 4. Esther Dyson

1. Leslie Bennetts, "Wired at Heart," *Vanity Fair*, November, 1997 p. 162.

2. Ibid., p.164.

3. Ibid., p. 167.

4. Claudia Dreifus, "The Cyber-Maxims of Esther Dyson," *New York Times Magazine*, July 7, 1996, p. 16.

5. Ibid., p. 18.

6. Esther Dyson, *Release 2.1: A Design for Living in the Digital Age* (New York: Broadway Books, 1998), p. 29.

7. Rana Dogar, "Deconstructing Esther Dyson," *Working Woman*, February 1998, p. 50.

8. Ibid., p. 48.

9. Bennetts, p. 166.

10. Ibid., p. 162.

11. Dogar, p. 48.

12. Dyson, p. 25.

13. Ibid.

14. Bennetts, p. 164.

15. John Gerstner, "The Civilization of Cyberspace," *Communication World*, June 16, 1998, p. 37.

16. Dyson, p. 40.

17. Bennetts, p. 167.

18. Ibid.

19. Ibid., p. 162.

20. Dogar, p. 48.

21. Dreifus, p.19.

Chapter 5. Steve Jobs

1. Owen W. Linzmayer, *Apple Confidential: The Real Story of Apple Computer,* Inc. (San Francisco, Calif.: No Starch Press, 1999), pp. 87–92.

2. Lee Butcher, *Accidental Millionaire: The Rise and Fall of Steve Jobs at Apple Computer* (New York: Paragon House Publishers, 1988), p. 16.

3. Butcher, p. 32.

4. Ibid., p. 66.

5. Linzmayer, p. 66.

6. Jim Carlton, *Apple: The Inside Story of Intrigue, Egomania, and Business Blunders* (New York: Times Books, 1997), p. 13.

7. Brent Schlender, "Three Faces of Steve," *Fortune,* November 9, 1998, p. 96.

8. Linzmayer, p. 242.

Chapter 6. William H. Gates, III

1. Bill Gates, *The Road Ahead* (New York: Penguin Books, 1996), p. 1.

2. Ibid., p. 12.

3. Ibid., p. 12–13

4. Ibid., pp. 2, 134.

5. James Wallace and Jim Erickson, *Hard Drive: Bill Gates and the Making of the Microsoft Empire* (New York: John Wiley & Sons, Inc., 1992), p. 35.

6. Stephen Manes and Paul Andrews, *Gates* (New York: Touchstone Books, 1994), p. 21.

7. Wallace and Erickson, p. 61.

8. Gates, p. 16.

9. Ibid., p. 17.

10. Ibid., p. 17.

11. Ibid., p. 45.

12. Wallace and Erickson, p. 126.

13. Manes and Andrews, p.128.

14. Ken Auletta, "Hard Core," *The New Yorker*, August 16, 1999, p. 61.

15. James Romenesko, "Bill Gates Sr. Can Take a Joke," *St. Paul Pioneer Press*, July 5, 1999, p. B1.

16. Jim Lehrer *Online News Hour*, PBS, June 7, 2000, <http://www.pbs.org/newshour/bb/cyberspace/jan-june00/statement_gates_6–7.html> (June 20, 2000).

Chapter 7. Steve Case

1. Joshua Cooper Ramo, "How AOL Lost the Battles but Won the War," *Time*, September 22, 1997, p. 49.

2. Amy Cortese and Amy Barrett, "The Online World of Steve Case," *Business Week*, April 15, 1996, p. 81.

3. Ibid., p. 82.

4. Alan Deutschman, "How Sibling Rivalry Created AOL," *GQ*, August 1997, p. 93.6

5. Cortese and Barrett, p. 82.

6. Deutschman, p. 94.

7. Cooper, Greenwald, and Krantz, p. 50.

8. Ibid., p. 49.

9. Judith Graham, ed., "Case, Steve," *Current Biography Yearbook 1996*, p. 81.

10. Ibid., p.80.

Chapter 8. Jeffrey P. Bezos

1. "Booked Solid," *People Weekly*, September 7, 1998, p. 70.

2. Jeffrey Davis, "The Poster Boy," Business2.0, June 1, 1999, <http://www.business2.com/content/magazine/indepth/1999/06/01/11440> (June 17, 2000).

3. "Booked Solid," *People Weekly*.

4. Ann Devlin, "Biography: Jeff Bezos," *Ann Online*, January 6, 1997, <http://www.annonline.com/interviews/970106/biography.html> (June 17, 2000).

5. Alan Deutschman, "The Amazin' Amazon Man," *Gentleman's Quarterly*, March 1998, p. 160.

6. Devlin.

7. Karen Southwick, "Above the Crowd: Interview with Jeff Bezos of Amazon.com," *UPSIDE Today,* September 30, 1996, <http://www.upside.com/texis/mvm/story?id=34712c154b> (June 17, 2000).

8. Ibid.

9. Ibid.

10. Ibid.

11. Ibid.

12. Ibid.

13. Davis.

14. Southwick.

15. Ibid.

16. Robert D. Hof, "We Want to Be the World's Most Customer-Centric Company," *Business Week e-biz,* May 21, 1999, <http://www.businessweek.com/search.htm> (June 17, 2000).

17. Southwick.

18. Jeffrey Davis, "The Poster Boy," *Business2.0,* June 1, 1999, <http://www.business2.com/content/magazine/indepth/1999/06/01/11440> (June 17, 2000).

19. Hof.

20. Ibid.

Chapter 9. Jerry Yang

1. William Plummer, "The World at Their Fingertips," *People Weekly,* December 4, 1995, p. 123.

2. Ibid.

3. "Winning on the Web," *Success,* February 1996, p. 27.

4. Amy Virshup, "Yahoo! How Two Stanford Students Created the Little Search Engine that Could," *Rolling Stone,* November 30, 1995, p. 16.

5. Ibid., p. 16.

6. Elizabeth A. Schick, Ed., "Yang, Jerry," *Current Biography Yearbook 1997,* p. 644.

7. "Winning on the Web," *Success*, p. 27.

8. Schick, p. 643.

9. Plummer, p. 123.

10. "Chief Yahoo," *Marketing*, October 30, 1997, p. 23.

Chapter 10. Linus Torvalds

1. Dan Gillmor, "How Finnish Programmer's Quest Challenged Microsoft and Made Him a Star," *San Jose Mercury News*, September 8, 1996, <http://www.newslibrary.com/ nlsearch.asp> (June 13, 2000).

2. Janice Mahoney, "The Mighty Finn," *Time*, October 26, 1998, p. 70.

3. Gillmor.

4. Rishab Aiyer Ghosh, "What Motives Free Software Developers?: FM Interview with Linus Torvalds," *First Monday*, March 1998, <http://www.firstmonday.dk/issues/ issue3_3/torvalds/index.html> (June 13, 2000).

5. Gillmor.

6. Chris Donohue, "Chat with Linus Torvalds," MSNBC, February 2, 1999, <http://bbs.msnbc.com/ bbs/msnbc-transcripts/posts/qk/276.asp> (June 13, 2000).

7. Gillmor.

8. Ghosh.

9. Donohue.

10. Ghosh.

11. Ibid.

12. Ibid.

13. Donohue.

Further Reading

Aaseng, Nathan. *Business Builders in Computers*. Minneapolis, Minn.: Oliver Press, 2000.

Byman, Jeff. *Andrew Grove & Intel Corporation*. Greensboro, North Carolina: Morgan Reynolds, 1999.

Dyson, Esther. *Release 2.1: A Design for Living in the Digital Age*. New York: Broadway Books, 1997.

Gaines, Ann. *Steve Jobs*. Bear, Del.: Mitchell Lane Publishers, 2001.

Heller, Robert. *Bill Gates*. New York: Dorling Kindersley Publishing, 2000.

Lee, John A. *Computer Pioneers*. Los Alamitos, Calif.: I E E E Computer Society Press, 1995.

Lesinski, Jeanne M. *Bill Gates*. Minneapolis, Minn.: The Lerner Publishing Group, 2000.

Northrup, Mary. *American Computer Pioneers*. Springfield, N.J.: Enslow Publishers, Inc. 1998.

Sherman, Josepha. *Bill Gates: Computer King*. Brookfield, Conn.: Millbrook Press, 2000.

Wolinsky, Art. *The History of the Internet and the World Wide Web*. Springfield, N.J.: Enslow Publishers, Inc. 1999.

Internet Addresses

Bill Gates
<http://www.microsoft.com>

Andrew Grove
<http://www.andygrove.com/> (Andy Grove's Website—
biography, speeches, and a virtual tour of his office and
Intel's virtual museum: how chips are made, how
microprocessors work)

Steve Jobs
<http://www.pixar.com/> (Pixar Studio's web site, with
information about Toy Story II)

Index